Dedicated to the memory of my parents

Set Your Soul Free

Do it, my friend
If it's your true will
Then nothing can
Stand in your way
Take heed to my words
When you lose your mind
Your soul will be free
Illusions will crumble
And then you'll find
The divine inside

My Poetry Life

I don't write any poetry
I've never done that
It's the coffee that does
I'm just along for the ride
But I've got these ideas
FUCKING grand ones
That are fueled by
Coffee and cigarettes

The Others

Ladies and gentlemen
And other assorted entities
We're all gathered here today
Because nobody else wants us
We are the others who
Roam the outskirts of society
Not fitting the ideas of normal
But we don't really care

Secrets From the Beginning

Thanatos, please come closer
And whisper in my ear
Tell me all the secrets
You have heard
From all the souls
You have collected
The secrets of humankind
From the beginning
Of our humanity

The Sacrifice

Carry me through
The unseen jungle
Beyond the realm of
Humanity, and all
Of their gods
And devils
As I sacrifice
Myself to myself
To gain wisdom

Water of Life

Pour me a glass of
The water of life
As we just vibe
With simply being

Self-Love

In order to
Really love yourself
You cannot hate
The experiences
Of your past
That shapes who
You are becoming

The Pendulum Swings

There is a certain perfection
Existing within imperfection
The true beauty of life
Because of its flaws
Light and darkness shift
As the pendulum swings
Continuously flowing
Master yourself and stand
On the point of balance
Flow with the current
While remaining unmoved

Dance Life Dance

Since time immemorial
Life danced with itself
Growing and evolving
Adapting to change
Through eons unimaginable
Fighting for survival
On this a planet, we call home
Flying through space

Just Flow

Let go of
All expectations
And just be
Flow with the spirit
Of creation
As your divine will
Directs your energy
Allowing you
To consciously
Create your own
Universe

The Hybrid

Aliens or witches
Which do you prefer?
Personally, I'd say
That I'm partial to
A red-haired
And tattooed
Hybrid woman

So, Blonds Have Fun

Whoever say blonds
Have more fun
May be onto something
But in my humble opinion
It's the redheads
Who add some
Spice to your life
They're simply better
In every imaginable way

Marshmallow Love

She smelled like
The sexiest
Marshmallow ever
It was almost
Unbelievable
And drew me into
Another world
Where love was
Not only playful
But also, kind

Flaming Locks

Oh, lady with
The flaming red locks
You set my heart
Aflame
My love for you
Is endless

Punk Rock Messiah

Sid Vicious
Died for our sins
But not
Of his own
Accord
It was a thing
Eris did to him
Before he
Could say no

Deadbeat Messiah

Psychotic dreams of
A deadbeat messiah
Are the only things
Keeping me sane
It's the last dance for
The angels of light
As a deadbeat messiah
Gives birth to galaxies

The Will

Ninety-three
He screamed
Do what thou will
With passion
And conviction
Then nothing
Can stop you

Walls of Time

As the walls of time
Collapse in on me
Angels dance on
My grave tonight
And my halo
Is losing its shine
Yet divinely
Inspired words
Still flow through me

Sleeping Goddess

I dreamed that my life
Was nothing but
A dream of a dream
Coming from the mind
Of a sleeping goddess
Reflecting all infinite
Possibilities from within
The center of the universe

A Moment of Zen

Barefoot and
Running free
In a moment of Zen
The stillness within me
Encompassing all
As the universe within
Mirrors the
Universe without

The Treasures

Scream
Like the mad
Without any
Supervision
You must decrease
Every day in order
To grow and
Find the true
Treasures of life

Furry Potatoes

Furry meat potatoes
Wheeking in unison
Knowing the hay
Will soon be refilled
Popcorning in delight
And zooming around
Their cage

What Are Words?

Words try to quantify
What cannot be known
By the rational mind
The truth of reality
Goes beyond the names
We use to identify
And categorize everything
There is no separate
This or that anywhere
All is a unified one

The Universal Language

Listen with your heart
To the universal language
That speaks directly
From soul to soul
Beyond any words
Just feel the energy
As it washes over you

Selfies and Enlightenment

The road to enlightenment
Is found in taking
Lots and lots of selfies
The clearer the picture
The more you will see
Beyond whom the world
Wants you to be
'Til you see your true face

Femme Fatale

She looked at me
With a sarcastic grin
That's when I knew
Trouble was coming
From this magnificent
Example of a femme fatale

The Flowing All

All is continually
Flowing and changing
Yet returning to
The same place
At a different point
Spirals and spirals
Weaving through
Reality like a
Universal DNA
Containing everything
That will ever be

The Undeadly Sin

Give in to
The undeadly sin
And meet God
As an equal
Then claim your
Own divinity

Flying High

I tried to fly too close
To the sun and burned
My soul away
Until it withered away
But I'm familiar with
This kind of pain

Guided by Love

Dance naked and wild
Beneath the full moon
Free in mind body and soul
Beholden to no one
Living life as you will
With only love guiding you

The Last Dance

Stare into the abyss
Of primordial chaos
As the Angels of light
Dance their last dance
And the whole
Of creation turns red
From the blood
They are shedding

The Heaven Within

In search of absolution
I blasphemed every
God known to humanity
To prove that I have
Moved beyond them
And freed myself from the guilt
Of the illusion of sin
I entered into the
Heaven within me

How Sure Are You?

How sure are you
That you know what
You think you know?
Look closer now
The closer you look
The more incomprehensible
Things start to be
What was no longer is
Look close enough
And words are no
Longer of any use

The Center

I stand in the center
That is everywhere
Searching for a circumference
That can't be seen with the eyes

Sweeter Together

Cupcakes and redheads
Two things that
Go well with each other
It's an exquisite combination
Unlike any other

Ballad of The Bulletproof Poet

The world is a cruel place
But I'm not afraid
I've got my armor
I'm a bulletproof poet
I've been through some dark times
I've been through some hard times
But I always find my way
I always find my way
To the light at the end of the tunnel
And I always find my way
To the other end of the tunnel
No matter what life throws at me
No matter what life throws my way
I'll always find my way
To the light at the end of the tunnel
And I'll always find my way
To the other side of the tunnel

I'm Going Mad

I can't take it anymore
I'm going insane
I need you to save me
I can't do this on my own
I'm losing my mind
I'm losing control
I need you to help me
I can't do this on my own
I'm losing my grip
I'm losing my hold
I need you to catch me
I can't do this on my own
I'm going crazy
I'm losing my mind
I need you to save me
I can't do this on my own

My Red-Haired Beauty

She's a red-haired tattooed beauty
And I love her with all my heart
She's got a rebel spirit
And a wild side that never quits
She's my tattooed beauty
And I'm never let her go
We'll ride together forever
Inseparable, we'll always be
She's my red-haired tattooed beauty
And I love her with all my heart
She's got a rebel spirit
And a wild side that never quits
She's my tattooed beauty
And I'm never let her go
We'll ride together forever
Inseparable, we'll always be

The Void

In the beginning
There was only darkness
And it was void
And it was cold
And it was empty
And it was dark
And it was lonely
And it was scary
And it was depressing
But then you came along
And you filled the void
With your love and your light
And your warmth and your compassion
And your understanding and your kindness
And you showed me that I was not alone
And that I was not afraid
And that I could be happy
And now the darkness is gone
And the void is no more
And I am no longer scared
Or lonely or depressed
Because I have you in my life
And you make everything better
And you are the light in my life
That guides me through the darkness

Red-Haired Queen

My red-haired queen inspires the best in me
She's my reason to be, she's my everything
I never thought I could feel this way
But I do, I do
When I'm with her
I feel like I can do anything
I feel like I'm on top of the world
She makes me feel alive
She makes me feel like I can fly
She makes me feel like I'm the best that I can be
I never want to lose her
I never want to be without her
Because she's my everything, she's my queen
And I love her with all my heart

Scream

I can't take it anymore
I'm losing my mind
I'm going insane
I need to let it out
I need to scream
I need to let it all out
I can't hold it in anymore
It's too much to take
I can't take it anymore
I need to scream
I need to scream like the mad
Without any supervision
I need to let it all out
I can't hold it in anymore
It's too much to take

Addicted

I'm addicted to the pain
The way it makes me feel alive
I'm addicted to the suffering
The way it numbs my mind
I'm addicted to the darkness
The way it engulfs my soul
I'm addicted to the emptiness
The way it makes me feel whole
I'm addicted to the alcohol
The way it numbs my pain
I'm addicted to the drugs
The way they make me feel sane
I'm addicted to the self-destruction
The way it makes me feel alive
I'm addicted to the self-hatred
The way it numbs my mind

What A Pain

What a pain
What a pain to make it to the end
Just to feel good again
If I had a dollar then who'd I thank
The Queen of Spades
More than anything I've paid
What a rage now it's just that I've never been so total
What a pain now it's just that I've never been so total
Yeah, I can't run, can't run, can't run, just can't run anymore
Tries to walk me right, starts to try and drag me under
Stays beside me just barely eighteen

I Can Hold You Now

You made me feel like I am a stranger
I can hear your voice in the dark
And I am just a tiny speck of light
You make me feel like a tiny speck of light
You made me feel like a tiny speck of light
I wish I could go on
But I can't make it without you
And I am living without my love
I can't make it without you
And I am living without my love
But I am living without my love
And I am living without my love
But I am living without my love
I can't make it without you
I can hold you now
I'm living without my love
I can't make it without you
And I am living without my love
But I am living without my love

There's A Healing Sun

I've got the urge
Cause there's no way I won't try again
I see it in my bones
I'm the one who's alone it seems
But if I see you smiling at me baby, you'll see me
'Cause you're the only one
I've got the urge
Cause there's no way I won't try again
I hear your voice
By the side of the street
The scars that you left behind
There's a healing sun
There's a healing sun
There's a healing sun
There's a healing sun
I can feel the flames that burn
Into the flame you've claimed
You can't do it
It's too late to stop

It's Our Job

It's so easy to fake a heart attack
Or to lose a little life back there
It's so hard to make love when your heart is bleeding
And so, nobody's business
But if you're really about love
Then you should know
And I don't want to meet your kin
Who are not making it a skill
It's our job
To help you out of this
Now your shoes are muddy, and you wear fake tears
And it's so easy to fake a heart attack
Or to lose a little life back there
It's so hard to make love when your heart is bleeding
And so, nobody's business
But if you're really about love
Then you should know
And I don't want to meet your kin
Who are not making it a skill
It's our job

To Live In

To live in
Where the people are
The best people, yes
Something I know
I might have made you cry
Or been the first thing that you see,
When I know you'll always stay
When I know that you'll always stay
You gotta think again
Then you'll have another chance,
You'll know you'll give it a chance again
The first time is the first time
When you're born into it
Then you're in it
And you should be,
Yes, you should be
I know you start with me
It's the last time that you know
I was never that proud at all
Then you see the world
That your mother had made
And even though they told you
There was more waiting

But Nobody Read One Page

I'm the one who got the monkey off my back
I'm the one who could make waves
That I don't make waves in my silly little world
My monkey is gone, and nobody knows
What he did with my tongue that day
He may have written a book of facts
But nobody read one page
So, I try to put my good mouth into my smile
Smiling people imagine what I'm thinking
Of Why I used to be funny most of the time
And how I deal with their jealousy
I'll get mad, but I don't like them when they come
And I wish I was her fairy tale princess
But all I know is I don't think it
That I like her just the same
And I like fairy tales just the same
And I like having lots of me

In This State I Am

Cause I don't wanna see you anymore
You know the way that you are
If you hurt me,
I will make up my mind
Go in some other direction
It's quite a good feeling
I am as free as a bird
In this state I am
I am as free as a bird
In this state I am
It's the same as singing in a movie
In a foreign land
Rain, rain, down and far
I am as free as a bird
In this state I am
I am as free as a bird
In this state I am
I gaze at the stars
Over on the horizon
I see the clouds again
And I see the fullness of the sky
Is there a cloud or a bright star

Fame And Glories by Moonlight

The goal
Is to find where you lie
And it seems, you're where that I'm
Somewhere in the distance you hear the snow crunching
You know it's great fun
Somewhere in the distance you see
The sound of a heartbreaker
You can hear the screams
From all the corners in the road
You know you're right there
The way those winter days can lead to one of
Fame and glories by moonlight
You can hear the wind across the mesa
The look in your yellow eyes
A look of pride tying
All those moments of true devotion
To your front door
And you know you're right there
The way those winter days can lead to one of
Fame and glories by moonlight
You can hear the wind across the mesa

Somebody New

In the eyes of a crowd
Where you can feel the music play
'Bout a month old
And I wonder if in this town
They're telling us
Somebody new
Dancing shoes, bang on your door
It's a real tight race
You look so happy, baby
But there's a hungry woman out there
There for you long last to you
Well, there's a hungry woman, so long last to me
I, I guess my name was Irreverent
And you know I wanna be with you tonight
Well, it's a long time ago
When I've known my baby for a week
And she doesn't answer
This might be the first
She's got her head in
Gonna be her last show
But I don't know

The Need for Show

I do have time for you,
I do have time for you
I do have time for you,
I do have time for you
I can't stop feeling this way,
I can't stop, no, no, no, no
I can't stop my arms from falling as they fall down,
So easily when I lay with you and you comfort yourself,
I'll, wanna be in tune with you.
I can't stop the feeling, the need for all the longing,
The feeling that the world hides,
The need for show.
I can't stop the feeling
It's that I don't want to hurt you
You know that its true
You don't want to hurt me
That's the hardest part
Just being inside your eyes

When We Kiss

You say you love me, am I wrong
Tell me what you mean to me
When we kiss
You're asking me to say that it's over
I say that it is
And it's good to know you're still love me
I want you to keep your faith, and not to cry 'cause I'll never let you
down
I've got a lot to give, from what I paid you
You know it's worth every grain of gold I can find, yeah
Cause I'm still with you
And I will always be with you
If we should say goodbye, I'll be glad to know
You know I'll keep your trust and it won't be like before
Can I come home
If you won't talk your life out with anyone

I Can't Believe Her

I can't believe her
There's not a single trace of a tear
I can't find the spark
And I can't lie
I feel like a fly in the eye
I get so mesmerized by her smile
I wanna see what earths made of pure illusion
I'm not quite so mesmerized
By any spark
I can't believe her
'Cause it's late and so many years gone
I've always dreamed I could love you
There's no love to find
You're a spark.
I've been busin' back and forth from my day job
To the world away to Paris or New York state so far away
The state of illusion is killin' me

Was It You?

Here I stand,
Wondering who you could be
What you could be
Was it you,
Was it you,
Were it you,
Was it you,
Whatever the reason
Whatever the reason
For you to believe me wrong
For you to believe me right
Here I stand,
Wondering who you could be

You, You, You

My world, my world, your world is still the same,
No one has ever walked through its many gates
Just another stranger in your life
You, you, you.
Just another stranger in your life.
Another stranger in your life
Just another stranger
Just one who tries to make it on his own
Is someone like you who don't see the truth about
Your loved one
I'm not so sure that
What I already know so real
My world, my world, your world is still the same
No one has ever walked through the many gates
With nobody ever really touched a human soul
Just another stranger in your life

A Little Too Close to Me

On Sunday afternoon, you're walking right by me, right now.
I'm feeling alright, I have a good time, I'm just miles away.
On the day we said the love's over, it was the best love of the year.
I'm under your spell, now it feels like years.
I can feel you when the lights are dimmer
We're all just hangin' by your side, yeah, yeah.
I'm under your spell, now it feels like years.
I can feel you when the lights are dimmer
We're all just hangin' by your side, yeah, yeah.
I know that you are standing there
A little too close to me
But I'm in a world of one and one with you

Let Me Down

When I was just a little boy, I never loved you too much
Yeah, I get all the love in the world and it's only bringing me down
My heart keeps saying goodbye to you and I'm just leaving
You let me down
I just don't get it
I'm walking on the run
Gone are the days
You let me down
Sometimes I wish I'd left
Other people's dreams
For mine instead
And I watch the way we're shaking
As I leave it behind
We're never apart
Never alone
I'm not going to live it up again
Except when someone loves me too
Like I need you
Remember when I once held you in my arms
Then I couldn't beg you to change
And dreamed of the places, I've grown
Believed I'll find someone

Maybe Just a Matter of Time

You're gonna love me more each time you begin to dream
And I will be strong, tonight with you
I can't remember the last time you warned me not to cry
I was down at the Senior; you could see me crawl
You looked so beautiful, you came and took me away
And the sun was coming up all the time
I don't want to live in a world of green
There must be a way to get to you
You never did tell me what to believe
I was down at the Senior; you could see me crawl
You looked so beautiful, you came and took me away
And the sun was coming up all the time
Maybe just a matter of time
I don't want to live in a world of green
I don't want to live in a world of wrong

Hell No

I'm just a bit wary though
You know I'm not a bad guy
Can you keep me sane
He was a man
From the outside looking in
All he had to give was a ticket
Takes a chance and then he gives up
And he shuts out the pain
He opens his eyes
He shuts out the pain
When he's alone, he doesn't feel
Like a boy
He's just a man
What makes you think you're a fool
I was lucky just to be born today
With the things you never asked me to
I didn't mind the working out
You thought my eyes were bleeding
Was it all a game?
Hell no
Why you no longer think about
All the things that you've said
No, I would not do

Try For Love

Oh, don't say you love me
I'll pay you the rest
You're gonna pay me the rest
Just try for a kiss
'Cause I'm such a fool
Now I understand
That love is here to stay
It is true
Love is here to stay
It is true
Love is here to stay
Why don't you try?
Try for love
'Cause I'm such a fool
Now you know
I know it's true
Love is here to stay
Don't you want it?
Try for love
I'm such a fool
'Cause I'm such a fool
And if you love me
Try for love
Laying on a beach all by myself.
I'll pull my blue jeans through your shirt

She's A Wild Woman

She's a wild woman
She's an actress
She's funny, she's exciting
She's a wild woman
She needs lots of care
She gets mad at me
She's such a wild woman
Who just wants to touch and touch alone
Someday, she'll teach herself to fly
Woman, woman, woman, woman
Well, I know she will
Look out across the sea
And there we'll start out to see
And watch a sunset burn white
And we'll hold each other tight
And we will fight
And we will run, and we will fight
And we will hold each other tight
and we will fight, and we will fight
And we will hold each other tight
and we will fight, and we will fight
And we will fight, and we will fight

I Am Alive?

With your beautiful daughter
And one of your grandaddies for a ride,
But I'm alive, I'm gonna get me a brand-new jukebox
I'm alive, I'm gonna get me a gun
And I am alive
I'm alive, I'm gonna find a way to keep you free
I'm alive, I'm gonna get me my life
I don't know how you gotta leave me,
A part for me, for me, for me
Maybe part of me, for me, for me
But there's no way we win
I don't know why you gotta leave me,
A part for me, for me, for me
Maybe part of me, for me, for me
But there's no way we win
I don't know how you gotta leave me

You'll Never Know

It's a chance you'll take.

You're my golden child

Be a daddies first generation of women?

Be a few nice to a lot of money!

Don't you wish you had?

Oh, yes, oh, it was so fun

Oh, I can imagine

Where your life is going

Don't know

No boundaries!

Oh, you're my golden child

Be a daddies first generation of woman?

Be a few nice to a lot of money

Girl it's a lot

To expect nothing

When it looks like

It will be

You'll never know

Girl it's a chance

When it looks like

It will be

You'll never know

One of the things I always loved about you

I'm Alive

So glad that there's somethin' you can do
So glad that there's somethin' you can do, baby
Oh, I'm alive!
I'm alive!
I'm alive!
I'm alive
I've been waiting, always waiting
I've been waiting, always waiting
Waitin', always waiting
I've been waiting, always waiting
Waitin' on the town that I'm makin' along my dark nights through the
years
Waitin' on the crops that have grown since I left you baby
And all your thoughts so far gone dry than your tears to my heart
You said I'll live my life a simple life
I've been waitin' now
I've been waitin'

Wish We Could

How can I keep you in mind
With a love we've never seen born,
We'll be loving again.
In your hearts
We've always been
In your mind
It's going to be
The very first time you'll see
The very first time we'll be
In our arms
We can't let go
Wish we could
That's the way it had to be
With a love we've never been born
We'll be loving again
In your arms
We can't let go
Wish we could
That's the way it had to be
With a love we've never been born
We'll be loving again
In your arms
We can't let go
Wish we could
That's the way it had to be

I'll Say It

So, I'm gonna tell this dirty little lie
So, she sees when she needs me
And when I've been there before
How she does it is another tale
I'll try my best, try it for love
But I'm not gonna make it
I'm gonna take it to her, or let it show
I'm gonna hold her over me
And I'll say it
I'll say it
Because she'll know when to stop herself,
That she just can't let go
She's got to know that I'm only a friend
And that he's not the same by my side
So, I'm gonna tell this dirty little lie
So, she sees when she needs me
And when I've been there before
How she does it is another tale

No, I'm Just a Stranger

For everything but that
If she had a body
Maybe someone
There'd be nothing to her
That might notice
But I won't
No, I'm just a stranger
That I know but I'm not the only
No, I'm just a stranger
There's a woman next door to me
Who's crying over a photograph
I'd like to take it with me
But I'm out of town next week
So can't see you
And if I give you a signal now
We can walk or something else each night
I'd really like to see you
I'd really like to see you
If I gave you a microphone
If I could take it to the lips
Then maybe I'd speak without being heard
But I keep coming back

The Other Cheek

I wish you could do it again
I'm not here to pretend that you're wrong
You know you're right.
But you'll always get.
I was never meant to hear you say,
That it was something I'd done wrong
But I'd do it again this time
Yes, I did it again this time
Oh, oh, oh, oh, oh, oh, oh, oh
It's just why I'm bound to turn the other cheek
And you're tackin' it on the rail
It's just why I'm bound to turn the other cheek
And you're tackin' it on the rail
It's just why I'm bound to turn the other cheek
And you're tackin' it on the rail
The other cheek

Of Yesterday

You have gone away
So, we had a laugh and we both died
We had a laugh and we cried
The night before my death,
How that I should die
Of sorrow,
Now you've come to me
And you die alone
'Cause it came as such a great surprise
As I never or never not
You are the melody
Of yesterday,
And I can't believe my eyes
Your love
I never knew
It came as such a great surprise
As I never or never not
I am the melody
Of yesterday,
And I can't believe my eyes
My love
The tune is a joke
So, my name is for you
Now that I'm gone
All those plans
Lovers seek
One thing for certain

Baby You're My Life

Oh, you been out on the town
I been a fool around here
I've got 'em packed tight inside, baby
'Cause sometimes the ends don't meet, baby
And I hear about you
And I wonder do I ever get to see you
Treat me girl
It's alright to go down
And into your dark night
Till I see you come home again
You're all that I need
And it's ok for me to let you go
All that I'm saying
Is simply that you're the only one for me
Baby you're my life
All I want, all I need
Baby you're my life
Just another night in heaven
Everything's all right
All that I want, all I need
Baby you're my life

Swimming In a Well

We were in paradise
When the waves came to stop their sinking
We were in heaven
When the waters turned gentle
We were in deep then calm
Just a band of retired flies
Swimming in a well
Were we in the good old New York
Oh, we were in heaven
When the waves came to stop their sinking
We were in the good old New York
Oh, we were in heaven
When the waters turned gentle
We were in deep then calm
Just a band of retired flies
Swimming in a well
Were we in the good old New York
The water was red, white and blue in the summer
But the water was still blue and grey
When the waves came the waves
And the wave
Weren't on the shore
The waves came the waves

If This Pain Ever Returns

They'll just go to waste
Like glue on your fingernails
If this pain ever returns
You'll just turn away
They'll just go to waste
Like glue on your fingernails
If this pain ever returns
You've heard all of the rumors
And yet I still find the same
These words came twice in one shock
Like a chain reaction taking place
We've heard all of the talk
But now I hear nobody works
Like the words on the screen
Lie on your back in the rain
Lie on your back in the rain
No, I'll be fine
All right
I'll be fine now it's going to be fine now
I feel the heaven inside me
And the angels play the hot light stories
But the show gets cut again

When You Stay

I think you're losing sleep
And then it hits me
When you walk away from me
Can't get over the feeling
Of you hurting so much
I hope it doesn't hurt me too much
When you stay
And sometimes it seems I can't get enough
Just my broken heart
Lately everything is shattered
It just like a shattered glass
There's nothing more to me
Every day I wake up with a look in my eye
These were the moments I was 9 years my old
Guess I was the best, were the best were nine, nine, nine
Were the best were five, nine, nine
Inside I know everything was caused by
The same guy that I heard about for the first time
Ten, nine, nine
No way were the work from where I started

That's My Nature

And I hear it
And in my mind
I can see the words I need in my mouth
Singing on my radio
And I can't stay there anymore
No, it ain't the same old place again
Cause it's hard enough just to let go
To leave what you're doing, and go where you're going
There's just so much more I wanna grow, in everybody else
Cause I wanna be the one who makes you happy
That's what makes me happy
Everybody look in my face, I wanna be the one who makes you smile
I don't have to shout it, no, I don't have to
I don't have to say it
'Cause honestly, babe, I just don't wanna be
People say, I'll be true
That's my nature

It Will All Be Alright

It will all be alright
Ain't there anyone else out there?
I'm walking with her tonight
It's a bit of a cross town contradiction
I guess everybody must have some local sympathy
But I'm home tonight from the Lower East Side
And I'm singing songs about James Dean
It all falls apart this time when I see her go
I am walking with her tonight from the Lower East Side
And I'm singing songs about James Dean
It all falls apart this time when I see her go
Maybe I'm a bit of a prodigal son
I been singing about James Dean
And maybe this whole thing has just begun
I am walking with her tonight from the lower east side
And I'm singing songs about James Dean
It all falls apart this time there when I see her go

I'm Getting Nervous

I'm never gonna make it home
For Christmas time is when the things we need most come unglued
We buy fancy clothes and dance in the snow
Time turns the lights off, we buy our second home
And get married in our limousines
I'm never gonna make it home
For Christmas time is when the things we need most come unglued
I'm never gonna make it home
For Christmas time is when the things we need most come unglued
I'm never gonna make it home
For Christmas time is that much fun
I know you're making me nervous,
But I'm giving you room to breathe tonight.
I'm getting nervous
And I know that you've been playing catch with me,
I'm nervous too.
I'm nervous too

I Guess I Made You Cry

It's alright, all you got to do is call and leave a message
Just be myself to keep you warm
I only want to see you, when you belong
I guess I made you cry
I guess I really care for now you know, I'm not a bore
I guess you'd think that I was the last man standing
Well, if you wanna come back to me, it's gonna be plain to see
I guess I misjudged again, and I'm gonna try again
With a vengeance and a second chance
All the women said "baby, it's none of your business"
But then I saw you coming that were all dressed in
Black and turquoise and doing with it what they could
I didn't know it would mean so much

Before It Rains

I ain't got nowhere to go
Don't want no place to go
Keep your faithless eyes off the wall
Let's get out of this town
Before it rains
And puts some pressure on the ground
Like a king who can work or let go
Keep your faithless eyes off the wall
Like a king who can work or let go
Keep your faithless eyes off the wall
Let's get out of this town
Before it rains
Run away and dry your faces
All my thoughts, keep you from madness.
I know what you think, don't get me into your plans
So, I can be sure that you really care

For Me

For me (for me)
When I need,
I need you there with me
And when I call
I always know the time is right
For me
For me
If you let me
I will never let you go,
And I will never call,
You will never have to say goodbye,
You will never have to say that
You love me,
Till you treat me right,
Till your life is done.
I love you
And I will be
I will never let you go
I will need you
'Til your love is gone
I love you
I can't let you go!
I love you
I will be
I will never let you go,
I will need you
'Til your love is gone

It's Just a Couple of Days

It's not the end of the world,
It's just a couple of days,
I never thought that I'd be without you.
I'm tryna take away the pain.
I'm tryna take away the pain.
I'm tryna take away the pain.
I'm tryna take away the pain.
I've got a little something for you.
I've got a little something for you.
I take it hard, every time I hear you on the telephone.
I got a little something for you.
I've got a little something for you.

I've Been So Lonely

You can have me, baby, 'cause I'm yours
Baby, baby, I'm so into you.
It's been so long since I've seen you.
I've been so lonely.
Now that I've found you.
You got my heart as hard as gold.
And my soul as raw as new.
And my love as old as time.
Now that I've found you.
You got my heart as hard as gold.
And my soul as raw as new.
It's been so long since I've seen you.
I've been so lonely.
Now that I've found you.
You got my heart as gold.
And my soul as old as time.
Now that I've found you.
You got my heart as old as time.

All I've Got

I'm not afraid of being with you
It's just the sound
Of a million voices
I'm not a child anymore
My songs have no backing
There's a place for me and you
And the world I bring
Has no place for me and you
I'm still learning.
Forget the sadness
And never give in
It's all I've got.
The feeling is it's alright now
It's all I've got.
The feeling is it's for sure (it's sure)
It's for sure (it's for certain)
It's for certain (it's for certain)
It's for certain (it's for certain)
It's for certain
I'm not afraid of being with you
It's just the sound
Of a million voices

I Can't Give It Up

You'll never know,
But love is a thing that can change.
I know, I know, I know,
How could I be so blind?
I am just a face that you can see.
I never saw how your love,
Could change your life.
And now I've seen how much is there in your smile.
I can't give it up
No, I can't give it back,
I'm noticing a wish to see you again,
And even if you give me a reason,
I can't give it up
No, I can't give it back,
I'm noticing a wish to see you again,
And even if you give me a reason,
I can't give it up

When Everything

Is getting stronger
Telling me that life is getting easier
I feel like a prisoner in a cage
And I won't let go
I know you've been taken
If you need someone
I'll reach for your hand
It's not your cup now
It's ours to fill
'Cause we want to be the ones
When everything
Is changing at the local, state, top speed
I can hear a man with a cowbell
He makes you laugh
When he sees you going
He tells you that you're gonna
Should've said the things that you need to say
Now, it's never enough, it's never enough
'Cause the closer you are the more
You can hear people on the street
Just pointing fingers
Being mean is never enough

Stop Crying

It's coming to me that we're waiting
Ain't nothing but good times
And I won't be sad to see you go
Or sad to see you go for good
You came back calling me repeatedly
Not like this just another time warp oh no oh no
In my year with you
I saw you passing your time without end
And though we may never meet again
I'd get by, I'd drop the knot and start over
So, stop crying
Stop crying
So baby, I know you feel the tears falling down my face
Cause it seems to hurt too much too soon

Living Life Beside Your Own

You can't tell me
(Don't you tell me)
I don't have a clue
(Nobody wants to know you)
So, you love me
(I don't have a clue)
Baby I do
'Cause I've known you for long
The promises we make
Do you see what I see?
Living life beside your own
Living life beside your own
Do you see how you can change
Living life beside your own
'Cause I've never seen love
Don't you see?
Living life beside your own
And living life beside your own
Do you see how you can make it right?
And living life beside your own

Night After Night

I'm trying to sleep
Night after night,
A long, long, long,
Night after night
I don't wanna fight my loss
Wanna walk into the fight
I told you, "I'm a guy who wants to win"
You don't have to say it
That's your choice
You don't have to hide it
If you feel it
I will never fight for you
Ooh yeah, now
Night after night
A long, long, long,
Night after night
I won't fight for you
Oh no, I don't wanna fight
I don't wanna fight for you
Yeah now
Night after night
A long, long, long,
I don't wanna fight for you

Turn Away, Don't You Know

Love should never be wasted
Love is the only thing we need
So why do I resist temptation?
I believe I found a way.
I believe I found a way.
Just another day in a cornfield
The corn fields can be full of boring faces
It's hard in a cornfield, you always get angry
And tell me to watch out,
But I'm alive and that is what I believe.
And it sure feels good, to turn away
Turn away, don't you know?
Turn away, don't you know?
It's just another day in a cornfield
I can plan it out, make it fit my imagination
I cannot stay for just one more day
In a cornfield
I try to stay out of your way

Every Day

I'm gonna be strong and free
I got my freedom
I'm gonna be strong and free
I can't take our love away
Yeah, I got my freedom
I'm gonna be
I wanna be free
Every day
I want to be strong
I miss the Sunday after school
It's the only time you're ever around
Well, I was blessed enough to learn
Everything you said
And the pipes in my head are full of questions
Do those questions still
keep lingering?
Have they all disappeared?
Have all the bricks that rode on a river
All disappeared some days?
Yeah, I want to be free
I don't want to be alone
I don't know what beyond the walls
Living proof, it happens everyday
When the stars collide, it happens to me

Together, Forever, Always

I want to believe
It's the only way of knowing
Every secret you have is gone
As tomorrow will turn into something more
As today it will never be the same
As tomorrow it will always be the same
This is the moment I know
This is what I wanna be
I wanna face the future
I wanna find the right way
For this little life, I choose
The way it is
We can be the perfect dream
If we open our hearts just a little
No one else will ever know it
Just like a child will always be the way it is
We will be there forever and always
Together, forever, always
I wanna believe
It's the only way of knowing
I wanna believe, I wanna believe
It's the only way of knowing

'Cause There's Just You

It isn't just anything
It isn't just anything
I know that you won't stay
And I'll do anything
Just to leave you again, yeah
'Cause there's just you
And I'll do anything, just to leave you again
'Cause there's just you and I
There's just you
And I'll do anything
'Cause there's just you
And I won't leave you again
I'm dreaming of a white Christmas
Just covered with snow
I'll put a little letter on your door
I'll write 'em all in my own letter
A small note from your Santa
I'll write 'em all in my own letter
A letter, baby
Santa Claus is knocking on my door

Better Stop Now

Now that you're here tonight
I don't know what to say
Just when I don't know what to say
I go back inside of me
And it's clear
And it knocks me out
Better stop now
Just before I hit the ground
If you don't know by now
I'm already dead
With no hope of life
Just when I thought by now
I'm gonna find somebody
And it's clear
And it knocks me out
Better stop now
Just before I hit the ground
If you don't know by now
I'm already dead
With no hope of life
Just when I thought by now
I'm gonna find somebody
And it's clear
And it knocks me out
Better stop now
Just before I hit the ground

It's a Moment of Confusion

We're running out of gas
We're running out of time
It's getting hard for us to keep up
We're talking back to the moon
In this moment it's really easy
We're saving faces for the past
We're thinking of tomorrow
It's a moment of confusion
We're turning into the moon
We're talking back to the moon
It's a moment of confusion
We're talking back to the moon
(She's gone so long)
She's gone so long, so long
And she's gone so long, so long
It's a moment of confusion
We're talking back to the moon
(You put me on TV that summer)
(You put me on TV that fall)
And she's gone so long, so long

Someday You'll Be Asking Why

It's not the time to waste
It's not the time to wait
I wish that life was like it is without you baby
When I can run back and fetch you
We can run back and fetch you
You can run back and fetch me baby
Bless you baby, you can run back and fetch me baby
Someday you'll be asking why
You'll be begging me to tell you why
It's not the time to waste
It's not the time to waste
It's not the time to wait
I wish that life was like it is without you baby
When I can run back and fetch you
We can run back and fetch you
You can run back and fetch me baby
Bless you baby, you can run back and fetch me back

I Got Broken

I said I'm not gonna take it back
I am not gonna say the things I said
I'm not gonna sit and wonder why that's true
The way that I look at you
I thought that you were the best that I had
But you turned away and then another part
You said that you didn't care I tried to change that
And when I was away the best things were still you
I got broken
Maybe you were more than just broken
I'm gonna leave you
So, if the sun goes down yellow sun and goes away, yellow sun goes
away
I see the white lies of beauty
And when I look into your eyes I see
The truth that lies underneath you
I'd spend all of your time trying to find
Just this one moment to survive

Ooh Yeah

To live in the city streets
No need for the courtesies (to see you there)
I see you standing there
Watchin' the crowd
Well, that's right, no need for the judge
You know, its heaven, no need for me to cry (that's right)
I want you
Love to love
Keep your latest story
Show me how
Don't need me
No need for the rain to fall
(That's right, no need for the rain to fall)
Ooh yeah
Babe, I know what that's like
Like you know
How the hunger pulls on you
Where I never thought you'd make it
Cause you need me
Need for living in the city streets

When You're Kissing Me

Cause I'm on fire
Cause I'm on fire
I know it girl
I'm on fire, girl
When you walk into the room
I can tell when your clothes are torn
When you're kissing me
Just by the color of your skin
I get the impression you feel me on the tip of your tongue
If I could only see the key
I guarantee that you'll say
When you're kissing me
It could be your name,
It could be your first name,
It could be your other last name,
It could be your photograph
It could be your fingerprints
Now I know it feels good
It's just a big party
You and me
Together for just one more night
Together for just one more night

I Thought I Was Home

I thought I was home
I thought I was somewhere new
But that didn't last me a day
Haunted by your smile
I thought I was somewhere new
But that didn't last me a day
Sunday drove away the moon
If only for a while
I thought I was home
And that didn't last me a day
But that didn't last me a day
I am so sick of you
I'm in such a hurry
There is nothing I can do
I need time on my own
I need to move along
I think I'm in for a bad night
There is nothing I can say
There is nothing I can do
There is nothing I can say
I hate to tell you this, I miss you so
But sometimes I dream I see you

The Things We Can Be

In our home, we will stay
And let your body let the secrets unfold.
And we will grow in our own way.
In the night, we will know
The things we can be.
And we will have new love.
In the night we can be so good.
We can turn the light up,
Just as long as we're in this moment
We can be so good.
We can turn the light up,
Just as long as we're in this moment
A world full of light,
A world full of shadows
A world full of words and
A world full of all.
The world full of light,
A world full of stars
A world full of love
A world full of fear.
We can come to learn.

Of A Seven-Day Day

Yeah alright
It's a time for compromise
And a race to the end
Of a seven-day day
There's only one way to go
And that's to put the hands of the races in the fire
A whole lot of pent-up frustration
In the heat of the day
You'd better do it all again
You got to work for change
Before this planet falls from day to day
There's only one way to go
And that's to keep it as long as you can live
The fight's still young
But it doesn't have to stop
It's a time for compromise
And a race to the end
Of a seven-day day
You gotta work on your feet, all the way
You got to work on your dreams, yeah
You got to stick together

Turn Away, Don't You Know

That love should never be wasted
That love is the only thing we need
So why do I resist temptation?
I believe I found a way.
I believe I found a way.
Just another day in a cornfield
And corn fields can be full of boring faces
It's hard in a cornfield, you always get angry
And tell me to watch out,
But I'm alive and that is what I believe.
And it sure feels good, to turn away
Turn away, don't you know?
Turn away, don't you know?
It's just another day in a cornfield
I can plan it out, make it fit my imagination
I cannot stay for just one more day
In a cornfield
I try to stay out of your way

Dreaming Of You

You made me love you
I'll never stop loving you
Baby, every time I think of you
I see it's enough for me
For love to cover the world
Oh, and now it's time to leave
Forgive and forget you and leave
Forget what you've done
I'm not worthy to you
And I know you're not worthy of me
All I know is what I feel
I'm just a memory in my mind
Dreaming of you
Tell me was it true?
When you called me
I was just dreaming of you.
All I know is what I feel
I'm just a memory in my mind
Dreaming of you
I gave you everything you never get

That The Night Was So Long

Cause, you know, your life is too
I was just a paper darlin' stick of drift
When my captain asked me to steer clear of his wife and kids
I knew we would not make his call and I knew
That the night was so long
That my captain thought I was gone
It was just a couple of miles down the line
So, I ran down, I ran down
(I ran down, I ran down)
Cause I knew, my life was too long
(Ohh oh oh, see a thing I miss)
(Ohh oh oh, see a thing I miss)
(I ran down and I ran down)
I knew it just wasn't fair,
To see my life just turned upon a distant horizon

I Think You're Crazy

I think you're crazy
You think that he belongs in a white haze
He belongs nowhere and his place is taken by rain
Everywhere he goes, he steals the hour and gets lost inside a cloud
I think you're crazy
You think that he belongs outside the blue
Tell me what can he do
I think you're crazy
You think that he belongs in a white haze
He belongs nowhere and your man is in cryin'
I think you're crazy and you think you're crazy
You think that he belongs in a white haze
He belongs nowhere and your man is in cryin'
If I could have the best white haze, then would it be me?
Do you know what I mean?
White haze, whitewash, white lies

And Now

Take me to the place
Where the moon is moonlight
And the stars are starlight
In this dream we know where to go again
Now, the place that I'm feeling
A dream that doesn't feel unkind
It's a space that I've traveled a million miles
And now,
I know where I'm headed
In this dream we know where to go again
So, take a good look at my handiwork
And how it moves across the bed
And how I long to see you in every dream
In this dream we know where we're headed again
Now, the place that I'm feeling
A dream that doesn't feel unkind
It's a space that I've traveled a million times
And now, I know where I'm heading

To Tell You

When you were young
Your eyes didn't hide
From the world,
When I look back at
The things I've done you
It shines in my eyes,
When I look back at you.
Don't try to save me
I've come to know you as
Your child
You left your life behind
You promised me
And you gave in to your loneliness so strong
I'm here to tell you
There are no secrets to keep
But I will try
To tell you
There are no secrets left behind
But I will try
To tell you
There are no secrets left behind
You left your life behind you
You promised me
And you promised me
And you promised me
And we both knew
One day, I'll make it all right

I Can't Give It Up

You'll never know,
But love is a thing that can change.
I know, I know, I know,
How could I be so blind?
I am just a face that you can see.
I never saw how your love,
Could change your life.
And now I've seen how much is there in your smile.
I can't give it up
No, I can't give it back,
I'm noticing a wish to see you again,
And even if you give me a reason,
I can't give it up
No, I can't give it back,
I'm noticing a wish to see you again,
And even if you give me a reason,
I can't give it up

All I've Got

And then I'm not afraid of being with you
It's just the sound
Of a million voices
I'm not a child anymore
My songs have no backing
There's a place for me and you
And the world I bring
Has no place for me and you
I'm still learning.
Forget the sadness
And never give in
All I've got.
The feeling is it's alright now
All I've got.
The feeling is it's for sure (it's sure)
It's for sure (it's for certain)
It's for certain (it's for certain)
It's for certain (it's for certain)
It's for certain
I'm not afraid of being with you
It's just the sound
Of a million voices

Together, Forever, Always

I want to believe
It's the only way of knowing
Every secret you have is gone
As tomorrow will turn into something more
As today it will never be the same
As tomorrow it will always be the same
This is the moment I know
This is what I wanna be
I wanna face the future
I wanna find the right way
For this little of a life, I choose
The way it is
We can be the perfect dream
If we open our hearts just a little
No one else will ever know it
Just like a child will always be the way
We will be there forever and always
Together, forever, always
I wanna believe
It's the only way of knowing
I wanna believe, I wanna believe
It's the only way of knowing

Stop Crying

It's coming to me we're waiting
Ain't nothing but good times
And I won't be sad to see you go
Or sad to see you go for good
You came back calling me repeatedly
Not like this just another time warp oh no oh no
In my year with you
I saw you passing your time without end
And though we may never meet again
I'd get by, I'd drop the knot and start over
So, stop crying
Stop crying
So baby, I know you feel the tears falling down my face
Cause it seems to hurt too much too soon

When Everything

When Everything
Is getting stronger
Telling me that life is getting easier
I feel like a prisoner in a cage
And I won't let go
I know you've been taken
If you need someone
I'll reach for your hand
It's not your cup now
It's ours to fill
'Cause we want to be the ones
When everything
Is changing at the local, state, top speed
I can hear a man with a cowbell
He makes you laugh
When he sees you going
He tells you that you're gonna
Should've said the things that you need to say
Now, it's never enough, it's never enough
'Cause the closer you are the more
You can hear people on the street
Just pointing fingers
Being mean is never enough

Can Forget About What's Going On

The world will never go on without you
So, take a look in these eyes of yours
And try to see through the romantic smile of shame
The things that you thought they'd never happen
Sometimes the world can be so confused
Can forget about what's going on
Can forget about all the stupid
Can forget about all the stupid
Can forget about all the stupid
Can forget about all the stupid
Things are so exciting, in the world today
Can forget about the future, in the world today
Can forget about birds and bees
Can forget about stars and the sky
Can forget about something, a dream
Can forget about everyone, in this life
Can forget about all, in this life
Can forget about all, in this life
Can forget about all the useless things

I Unlocked the Door

I'm still the same as before
But I won't fall in love anymore
'Cause you're the only thing that keeps me alive
Oh, so how can it be true
That I'm on my own now?
'Cause I've been waiting here for you
Deep in the night I fell
When there was light underneath the candles
I unlocked the door
And deep inside I fell in love
I know there's no one there
I know it's just a matter of time before I'm with you
And deep in the night I fell
When there was light underneath the candles
I unlocked the door
And deep inside I fell in love
I know there's no one there
I know it's just a matter of time before I'm with you
I'm not the same

Wake Up Tomorrow

I'm gonna ride into the night
And wake up tomorrow
I'm gonna wake up tomorrow
And you will see
My love is dead
If I'm gonna survive
I'm gonna ride into the night
And wake up tomorrow
I'm gonna wake up tomorrow
And you will see
My love is dead
If I'm gonna survive
I'm gonna ride into the night
And wake up tomorrow
I hate to wake up tomorrow
But this ain't the last time that we interrupt our great big world.
I'mma let you in my arms again
And even if it's not tonight
Love is just a state of grace
You divine it and then you're proof it
And I believe in love.
I'mma let you in my arms again
And even if it's not tonight

Everything Else Died

It's the end of the road,
And the end of that one-way highway,
And it's the end of this summer's hard road to recovery.
It's the end of this summer's hard road to recovery.
I remember I was six years old; you knew it too late
I turned your water dishes on the overload
Of the sad highway's steel wheels
I was alternative motel where you belonged
And everything else died
Let the overload eat you up inside of you
So long ago, everything was easy
Just a one-way ticket in time for a picnic
You could jump right in, you could try anything
But it ain't like me
And some of us ain't goin' out
Let the overload feed these tears inside your eyes

You Weren't There

With you and me
My heart is a little scared
I haven't seen you around
Lately I've been thinking how much I hate you
And now that you've come back, I'd be mad
I'd need to be mad
'Til I can be loved
You didn't mean to make me feel bad
I know you do but honestly
You weren't there
To hand me kisses
And make me feel guilty
I didn't mean to make this clear
All my broken hearts and my reasons
I'll prove to you how much I need you
There's nowhere I'd rather be
With you near and far between
I hope I don't turn back
The way that you decide
What it is we blame where we stand

Loud, Long and Nameless

Cause I ain't gonna waste another day
Loud, long and nameless
She came running on burgundy
Then she crashed her car to the ground
She's lost in that foggy cradle of water
Oh, she took a boat to Spain
Yeah, she took a boat to Spain
Gleaming feat, she kept on sinking
Wounded and spinnin' out of her head
She's spent years tryin' to stay on the shelf
She's tryin' to keep a little runny nose afloat
But still, she knows something is wrong
It's got a hold on me
And it's got a hold on me
When you see a whole bunch of hungry people
Standing around like dancing games
Well, you better end them runnin' around in circles

When Christmas Trees Are Bare

You're not the only one
Who wants to live in a time
When Christmas trees are bare
And we hear the Christmas song
But who wants to live in a time
When Christmas trees are cut down to ashes
And all our children starve
If we'd only buy those Christmas trees
Who wants to live in a time
When Christmas trees are bare
And we hear the Christmas song
But who wants to live in a time
When Christmas trees are cut down to ashes
And all of our children starve
If we'd only buy those Christmas trees
Now it's Christmas and it's how I spend it
And Christmas is the only time I see my son
Where the fires are lit at ten o'clock
But Christmas trees are cut and all of them
Have burned out.

When I'm Lonely

I'm a rebel
It's all about who you are
No one else can make you smile
All of my friends say you're the only one
When I'm lonely
And I need you
And there is nothing else
To give
All I need
Is for you to love me
All of my friends say you're the only one
When I'm lonely
And I need you
And there is nothing else
To give
All I need
Is for you to love me
All of my friends say you're the only one
When I'm lonely
And I need you
And there is nothing else
To give
All I need
Is for you to love me
All of my friends say you're the only one
When I'm lonely
And I need you

Empty Shell

I'm an empty shell of who I don't want to be
I'm a ghost of my former self
I'm a shadow of who I used to be
I don't know who I am anymore
I don't know what I want in life
I just feel lost and alone
But then I see you and I remember
Who I used to be
And who I want to be again
You make me feel alive
You make me feel like I can fly
You make me feel like I'm on top of the world
With you by my side, I know I can be who I want to be
With you by my side, I know I can reach for the stars
So please, don't let me go
I need you in my life
I can't do this alone
I'm an empty shell of who I don't want to be
But with you by my side, I know I can be who I want to be

If You'll Let Me, Baby

If you'll let me, baby
If you'll show me how, show me how I am, babe
And I will never be satisfied
If you'll let me, baby
If you'll show me how, show me that I am, babe
You're talking now about the man in the long neon yellow coat
Well, I don't see no reason to be sorry
I only want clothes and a little more
If you want me tonight, I ain't a fool
Though I'm trying to be so affectionate
And I don't care so much what goes on inside
If you see me coming and there's no one around
Tell me why, tell me why can't we just get used to it?
Tell me why, tell me why can't we just get used to it?

Come Hold Out

On the ground
Gonna take a chance
Come out your shadow
Swing for the beat
Take a chance
Swing for the beat
Come out your shadow
Hold on tight
To the beat
You're only a member of this song
Out of this world you fly
You're only a member of this song
Come hold out
Your love upon parting
You send peace on earth
This child of mine
Come hold out
Your love upon parting
You're only a member of this song
Listen live to me when I make a surprise appearance
At the ready
I just might make you shiver
With the sweet sound of my heart
And bring a peaceful soul
There'll be no earthquake
For there'll be peace upon the ground
There'll be no pain

Let's Leave This Chain Together

This day
And this evening
Don't worry about tomorrow tonight
But on a world, that's not broken
The sun will shine
It may not shine anymore
It may not shine anymore
So don't be shy
It's time to be free
'Cause my love is strong
Let's leave this chain together
Let's hold on to what we've got
Some more Saturday night
Now that I'm hanging over,
I don't know what tomorrow brings
Another day to go by
It's my time to get smart
I don't care if the answers never
Sound, or slide,
But I would do it, one more time.
It's my time to be free
'Cause my love is strong
Let's leave this chain together

I've Been Lonely Too Long

When you're older, you can see things look better
You can be the reason for the weather to change in the winters
I used to dream, you and I had a falling out
Then I realized your lonesome voice made that sometimes last
When I'm alone, I start believing it soon
You're not the same you used to be
I can still hear you whispering as far as I go
I guess I need some kind of answers
I'll think of you where we've never been
When you're older, you can see things look better
You can be the reason for the weather to change in the winters
I've been lonely too long
I've been sitting in the dark too long
And it's getting kind of cold again
I guess I need some kind of answers

If You Hurt Me Like You Should

You can't love me like I love you
And I ain't gonna cry 'cause you know I would, uh uh uh uh
I swear to you that I'll righteously say these words
If you hurt me like you should
I swear to you that I won't cry because you know I would, uh uh uh uh
I swear to you that I won't cry because you know I would, uh uh uh uh
I swear to you that I won't righteously say these words
If you hurt me like you should
I swear to you that I won't cry 'cause you know I would, uh uh uh uh
I swear to you that I won't righteously say these words
If you hurt me like you should
I swear to you that I won't righteously

I Can't Let You Go

Are you living with me
Where the sun goes down so fast
I'm standing by the side of the road
No one to ask you to dance
Is it me you're walking the street
All that darkness with everyone
Is it you you're changing the channel
I'm out in the cold all the time
When I close my eyes it's you, I see
I have been lost for so long
I can't let you go
I can't let you go
When the wind has knocked me all around
I must say I can't believe
I feel so good in my mind
The sun in the grey sky no stranger happens in my town
'Cause it's me and you there, yes, they are
And the same old hunger in my eyes
Yes, I believe it's me

That You Last

I thought I had things all figured out
But I was mistaken
When I said I love you
I wasn't as sure as before
In your junk dog eyes
I never thought I'd die!
Don't ask me why it was
I can see through the
There's something deep inside
And it's just something deep inside of me
Don't ask me why it was
That you last
Why don't you ask me
Don't you ask me why it was
Somewhere on the rise
There'll be blue eyes
And a mystery in me
Warm to the touch of your hand
Lay your head on my bed
Don't you want me, want me
Don't you see myself fading away

'Cause You're My Everything

I will be your voice
I will be your star
I will be your best friend
You're my only friend
I will be your everything in life
All I do is keep me warm
You're my everything, with you in my life I'm waiting
For you in every way I conceivable
And you know that I've waiting
For you in every way everyday
As I work my body, fighting the feeling
Of running and lifting a rock
You're my everything, with you in my life
I'll get my lady, girl right here
And right behind too
It's my way of living
'Cause you're my everything
And I can't feel painin' down at sea
'Cause you're my everything
And I can't feel painin' down at sea

That You Won't Deny

You'll be a part of
Some say you've never had
A true love affair
And you're a man
And it's this love
That you won't deny
No, it has never been
And it's this love
That you won't deny
I thought that I heard you calling
And a I knew that you were a liar
But it's all a lie
So put your ear close to the phone
And your voice is right
Come out and say that you're in touch
Don't make this such a dream
We live and dream and then we die
And it's all a lie
We live, and we dream but
The world moves and sometimes it doesn't know
And it's all a lie
And it's all a lie

Crazy Woman

I don't really want to change your mind
'Cause you're the only one Who'd ever want something more
Even if it's more than you give
I'll give you something that will bring you down
I'll give you what you need babe
It's no big deal if you give
I'll give you what you need babe
Crazy woman
She's a little bit mysterious
All I see is her eyes
And the things she says
Like ""let's go boy""
Will get you into bed
I'll give you something that will bring you down
Like a beatin' vocal
I play for fun, just for laughs
Does she get you to sing the blues?
She wonders comin' hard to find
She's cryin' in the yard

Love In a Groove

What do you think
All this is over, this is over!
So don't make me wait
I'm not in the mood anymore.
Love in a groove
Love in a groove
Love in a groove
Now you think about it.
Don't you get sentimental, honey
When you think of a girl who could
Do it, too
And end up in a commitment?
What do you think of it
All this is over, this is over!
So don't make me wait
I'm not in the mood anymore.
Love in a groove
We could have some magic
in the groove
What do you think of it
All this is over, this is over!
I've been thinking
All these years
I've been waiting

She's a Woman

In the shadow of her brother, she feels herself in my hands
She's a woman
She's a woman
(Well, anyway who knows but she's a woman)
Well, when they bargained with the devil in Heaven
They been selling everything that they could hope to give
Well, they were selling everything, what they got was snake oil
Some were pretty strong they could take everything
And mmmmm, who knows?
Well, no one knows really that long
'Bout that attitude, woman
If you love somebody like I do
You're gonna have to try for higher ground
Well, if you love somebody like I do
It don't make a difference if they love you back
It's just your soul that you have to release

I Wonder If You Know

It's only a matter of time before you find yourself
In every conversation, every line in every note
In every communication you must keep in soundbites and pauses
That will bring you closer to her
A world of meaning and understanding were
Someday gonna see what we're trying to find
I've just begun to think what the words really mean
In a world that looks like this
I've just begun to feel what the words really mean
Thinking with just one friend shows you the things to think about
Now that the reasons are clear it's clear why it's always easier to lose
yourself to desire
The more you know, the less you know
I wonder if you know
I wonder if it's really over
I wonder if I'm over the edge

I Spoke

I spoke
What did you think was right?
If I ever lose you
What will it take to keep you by my side?
And I'm coming home someday
I hope you're alright
Well, you and I just made our dreams come true
Thought we'd been through it
So many times, you put me through it
Never put me through it
I'm coming home once again
And I'm coming home once again
You thought that I was crazy
But I was surprised, oh, it blew my breath away
You thought that I had no tomorrow
But I was surprised (surprised now)
That you would come around
Oh, I'm coming home once again
And I'm coming home once again
Think I was through
So much has happened that never could happen

I Feel Okay

I'm looking for something
And I see you in a way
You really drive me crazy
This is the last time I'm giving you credit
All that I can give is a smile
I'd like to watch you go
These words sound trite, but they carry that appeal
You're the best girl I've ever had
You're the best girl I've ever had
You know I'm feeling alright
I feel okay
Don't put me in your sights
Girl I'm coming home
You do the driving, you do the backyard dance
You're the best girl I've ever had
You're the best girl I've ever had
You know I'm feeling alright
I feel okay
Don't put me in your sights
Oh, I'm coming home, leaving you alone to worry

It's Just a Little Bit

A bit of life
Baby, give me some
Some more
Just a little bit
(Baby) Little bit
(Ain't that a thing of the day, no)
No use
(Baby) No, no, no
It's just a little bit
(Ain't that a thing of the day no)
Don't leave me here to stay for life
It's just a little bit
(Ain't that a thing of the day, no)
You're just a bit shy
(Ain't that shy, no)
I know you play
(You play) with your toys
And I think it's lovely
Although there's no music
I know there's something new
Something new to hear
Something new to us
How did I get through

I Got Your Mother's Eyes

I got your mother's eyes
Don't tell me you're sorry, it's too late
I'm gonna get a baby and make my life stand forever
I got your mother's eyes
The secrets she kept secrets
All the love we had meant to one another
Every night I light a candle together
Have stayed up all day
I want to give to you
I want to share in this night
Somehow, I don't want to say goodbye
I got your mother's eyes
Don't tell me you're sorry
I was a little cold before the storm
But I'm not afraid of losing my wings
Though the seasons are changing, the changing of the changes
Of the colors changing, the changes of the sun

I'm The Man

But I love her
I can't help it if she were gone
I'm the man
I can't help it if she is gone
It's up to me
It's up to you
To take the fall if you feel so unsure
If you're feeling insecure too
I'm the man
You get the speech in your head
But sometimes it feels so disguised
All the things that you want and deserve
I'm the man
You get the speech in your head
But sometimes it feels so disguised
All the things that you want and deserve
I'm the man
I can't help it if she is gone
I can't help it if she is gone
You get the speech in your head
But sometimes it feels so disguised

You Got to Know

If I could do it all again
If I could do it all again
I'd have to work on my feet again
If I could do it all again
I'd have to lose control again
I'd be doing it all again
With every nickel that I have
With every nickel that I am
Every nickel that I am
If I could do it all again
With every nickel that I have
With every nickel that I am
I could do it all again
Then I'd have to try again
You got to know
You can do it all again
Every nickel that you have

Can't You See

You're right there
Can't you see
I'm so blind
You're the only one I love
I don't want you to change your mind
I just want you to be myself
And I can't take that chance
You're right there
Can't you see
I'm so blind
You're the only one I love
I don't want you to change your mind
I just want you to be myself
And I can't take that chance
You're right there
Can't you see
I'm so blind,
I'm so blind!
I'm so blind!
Don't go searching around
I'm the one for you,
Ooh, everyday
Everything leads me here inside.
Inside I believe in you!

Theories In the Sand

I thought I'd seen it all before
The writing on the wall
It's getting clearer
Can't believe that I'm trapped inside
The lies can't turn around
Can't believe there's something better
Can't believe I'm a loner
But that don't mean it's over
Can't believe the lies can't turn around
I can't take what I got
Can't believe we're forever
Can't believe anything that's written
Can (don't need to believe tabs)
Theories in the sand
Can't believe you know there's a way
Can't believe you know it's a lie
Can (don't need to believe tabs)
Theories in the sand
Can't believe you know the truth is lies in the sand

Love Shines Through You

When it's your turn
Love shines through you
Love shines like never before
So much to tell you
You'll always be the first to know
Like never before
I can't tell you
A lie
Love shines through you
Love shines like never before
I can't tell you a lie
Love shines through you
Love shines like never before
A song of new hopes
Love shines through you
Love shines like never before
A song of new hopes
(Ooh ooh)
(Ooh ooh)
(Ooh ooh)
(Love shines through you)

There Is

Gonna, show you how
We're gonna make it out
Gonna, make your heart come tumbling down
Gonna, make you feel the same as I do
I know from personal experience
There is a way
And you will see it in the way
Of the kind words conceal
And the kind words betray
Something in the air
Of the wrong kind words play
And it is one
And you will see it in the way
Of the kind words deface
And the kind words wound
I want to bury you in the deep
That it just couldn't hurt to bury you up this easy
You know I've known 'em but this is the story
About a flirt with his final defeat
I talked about the love that he gave me
I wanted to leave behind

I Don't Wanna Stay Here

(I don't wanna stay here)
My friend says I'm a total freak
We could let this dream fly
But there's something very wrong
Cause even now when I say I wanna stay here
I have to say I'm a little cruel
Cause it's not the words that make me hate
I have a picture of you here
And all my friends say I'm always bad
Don't like that, I want you bad
Don't like that, I want you bad.
You think that I'll find a way to make of your way
Like I always wanted you to be there
My heart, and it'll only show
My heart, and it's really true
I need you so bad
My heart, and it'll only show
My heart, and it's really true

Where Does the Time Go?

We got down and tired of living in the sun
Life had come a long, long, long before we came
And there was a place outside of a subway car
Oh, subway car
Where does the time go
Come on baby
My world has gone a long, long way
subway car in my pocket
Where does the time go
Nothing wrong with me
I see it all around me
Closed eyes, empty hearts
Closed eyes, empty hearts
Yeah, open up your eyes and open up your heart tonight
But let them let those closed eyes
Empty eyes, empty hearts, empty hearts
Empty eyes, empty hearts, even
Empty hearts down in the snow
Oh, subway car in my pocket
Where does the time go
Come on baby
There ain't no secrets any of them

Mississippi Highway

It's getting so dark
The street's crawling and
If you can, fight it
'Cause we were all born in the car crash
We lost control and drove out
We were warriors here on the run
We were born that night in the city
You never said not to think, we said it twice
And that was a twelve-ounce mess
That night in the club
I woke up in due time
Drove to my father's truck
Took a ride to the track
Mississippi highway
Knew him from the street
Well, we drove till we bailed
We fell we roamed the world
Drew into this dream
That it was your dream
I woke up to find
I knew you by the arms
I woke up with a feelin'

Until You Don't

It's not what I was sent here for
There's an unexpected twist
That just when goes terribly wrong
And I've tried to tell you
As much as I can
Until you don't
I'll miss you
And I'll miss you
Until you don't
I want you
I never meant to hurt you
And even though I know it's wrong
I never meant to hurt you sincerely
Even through our darkest hours
I know that you're still mine
I'll miss you
And I'll miss you
Until you don't
I'll miss
I'm sorry
I didn't mean to hurt you
I didn't mean just to hurt you
So, forgive me baby
You never meant to hurt me sincerely
And even though I know it's wrong

How To Make It Better

We'll take one day at a time
We'll try to make it better
Give us a piece of your mind
How to make it better
How to make it better
How to make it better
There's a place
Where you go
I'll walk with the snow
I'll win a bet
No matter what it takes
We'll stay warm in that warm home
Soarin' hot with the warmth of a home
I've got a dream for tomorrow
And I don't know when
We'll reach a place
Where the warmth is at hand!
I know you're waiting
And so, this must go
That you show me the way!
There is a place
That I've been to before
And I will follow where I went wrong
And I'll stand on the ground

They Can Never See

You're not afraid of what we can't see
We can always use our hands
But we can never show the world to someone like you
I'm scared of what the world will take
I'm scared of what the world is not saying
I'm scared of you, I'm scared of you, it's a shame
Gonna live in your dreams
When all the world falls in
No one here can hold me tight anymore
Don't want no comfort, I'm not scared enough
Baby here behind you
They can never see
No one here can touch me no, no
No one here can hold me tight anymore
Don't want no comfort, I'm not scared enough
Baby here behind you
They can never see
No one here can touch me no, no

It's Seven Eighty

I got your back
All I'm asking was for the love of our lives
Is this all we live
It was meant to be
My soul in the hands of time
Time is a winner boys and she came
And changed the world again
So, take a look now into this truly beautiful world
And look again tonight
And know we live in a different world
And we've only just begun
And she was no ordinary patient
But everyone's waiting tonight
For someone who doesn't fall apart tonight
It's the seven eighty
Yes, it's the seventy-nine
And it's seven eighty
Yes, it's the seventy-nine
And it's seven eighty
Yes, it's the seventy-nine
And it's seven an' it's a better life than the ordinary one
Get the best of me

I've Got to Try Someday

You're the only one
Just a little bit of love will bring you back
I guess I could help you live your life
I never heard a single one of those people
Oh well I've got to try someday
I know it could be wrong
I know there's no one to turn to
But I hope that you know that
I've got to try someday
I know it could be wrong
I know there's no one to turn to
But I hope that you know that
I've got to try someday
It's not too late
To find a way to get you off my back
I don't want to live without you babe
Don't want to be without you
I don't want to be without you
I didn't tell you I wasn't fancying you

Your One Desire

I'll never stop loving you
It might be a long road ahead
I know we'll meet again someday
You're the rock you're the one
Will you come back tomorrow
Will you face the unknown
Sleeping with a ghost, you're my one desire
You take my heart and walk it back
You give me strength to live on
Is there time for you to go away
Is it too late to try
To give this foolish thing one more try
As the time of our lives
We stare at the dark
Your one desire
I can make it better
I can make it my own
You make the noise and walks
And you make my heart sing
I must confess that I'm not alone
I know I'm not fooling anyone

For A while

You're gonna see what they say
I think I'm gonna love you for a while
You're gonna see what they say
I want you for a while
You're gonna see what they say
Don't take my advice
It's very, very foolish
You gonna see what they say
You're gonna love
For awhile
For a while I thought I could rise above
But I'm locked in a cage and I'm clinging to a ceiling so high
And I can't let you down, can't let you down
But I'm trying, but I'm trying
I'm a lonely soul
Needin' to be free is what I want it to be
Needin' to be free is what I need it to be
I need a place to hide away

For Prove

We're all fools
You won't stand for long enough.
So just take my word
That it's not enough
For prove
We want what we lack
Just to have it all...
Well, I'm tired of being tired
But I need some action tonight
Would you like to play a part?
To help me understand
(it's not like I) how I needed to be treated
The way that you wanted me believed
In our common good (yeah)
We fought like dogs to keep the love alive
(You see) (yeah)
And you wanted our love alive
(it's not like we fought)
It's not like we became the same
(Oh, feel the love.)

So Complete Without Your Woman

It's got me by surprise
No two ways about how we feel
I guess everything goes bad (I'm so alone)
Now you're all alone
And everything goes bad (I'm so alone)
Close your eyes and you will be alright
Nothing to fear, nothing to fear at all
And you will be so fine
You've got so many things to worry about
And you must care for me
You're everything that's all and nothing
So complete without your woman
You're everything that's all and nothing
And just the thought of you
We're on top of the world
And darling just thinking of us
You're everything that's all and nothing
And you're thinking of me
You're everything that's all and nothing
So complete without your woman

That Says

We'd give it everything we had before
If each rose were in our garden
So, tell me before the sun comes shining
If each kiss could rise even higher
If I could have every single beat, you give
Baby I could
If she were alive today
Would give all her love to me
'Cause a man just has to tell
That love can do so much for you
And I will trust in you again
Until the end of time
I want you baby
I want you little everyday thing
You've got a right to keep
A man has a right to keep
He's got to have a thing that he can hold down
For there's something deep in your soul
That says
If I should die
Baby I want you
I want you little everyday thing

Come Together

So far, I've waited
For something to come along
That'll bring me home
And make me feel complete
I don't care just wait
'Cause I'm closer than I've ever been
And I'll be so proud
When I touch your hand
I'll be waiting I'm waiting
When I touch you your hand
I just can't stay
And feel the love flow
And come together
I've waited all this time
And now I'm living and dying alone
I'm in the strangest love
When I finally fall in love with you
It's almost like it could change my life
Such a simple thing to take place, baby
It could change my life
Like I want to stay
What would I do
Would I do it all over again

I Will Be Your Man

I know I want you (You want) (You want)
It just feels right
It doesn't make sense
It doesn't make sense at all
I will be your man
You're not confused
I will be your man
You're not like you
You're not like you
I am the kind of man
Who doesn't love you
You know, the kind of man
Who is afraid of being
I will be your man
I will be you're not like you
You're not like you
I am the kind of man
Who is afraid to
I will be your man
I will not like you
You're not like
I am the kind of man
Who is afraid to
You are now

You Should Have Known Better

You'll be better off without me
Won't be better without me
You should have known better
You should have known better
It might have sounded like a dream
You could have had it all
Show the world your eyes
Check out the things we are really afraid of
I know, I know, I know
And all the things we say
I'm gonna find me a real love
You're gonna get it, you're gonna get it
But you're not gonna get it in time
If I could just roll with the times

I Can't Wait Until Evening

I can't wait until evening
I am tired of living every day
I can't lose my taste in life as long as I live
I'm tired and bored of living any more
I need a new take in everyday
I need a body with a different name
I'm in hot water since you said you're no good to me
I'm just trying to get on your radar
I'll see you when I come down
When your gonna start surfin' around
I get a jitterbug on my side
And I gotta roll ya know with me
We can ride in the air in the rough

When You're Gone

Your name's on my wall
When you're gone
My whole world's changed
Don't give up
You can't get nothing back
When your everything is gone
If the girl that I love is gone
Don't give up,
You can't get anything back
It all seems so simple
Why don't you give me some more
How can you take away the pain
It's a very hard way
So hard to live, don't give up
Why don't you give up
It's a very, very good reason
Why don't you give up?
And in the name of Goddess, we'll meet again
Across the sky,
For in the name of Goddess, we'll meet again
Where we're not asking for our freedom

Future Youth

I got your heart for me, my man
I got your heart for me, my man
We got our time to find what matters
We got our future in mind
Future youth
Future justice
Future safety net
Future better times than yesterday
Future all time
I know I'll get over to you in a little while
I drove my daddy crazy
In a little time
And he always promised that he'd be true
He got a little boy to meet,
And he said he'd always remember you better than I do
And the road I chose was dark and rolling
And I did not know what to do
I know I'll keep my mind straight then
And I know that I'll keep my son
For if I had not got your heart for me

Now The Sun's Pounding Hard

You can see my heart
Now you're a hot thing
Now that something's getting young
Watch me try to watch you too
Now the sun's pounding hard
And it's crawling around you
And it's burning you back to the rock
You're the girl to watch out for
Now the sun's pounding hard
Don't you get to choose
No, you can't see all the sunny days
Don't you sleep with another lonely soul
Oh, we all sleep together
Now this house is a little colder,
The heat is gone
And I think it's time to brush up on speed
Fresh air and a big hood
I've got a lot of room, so let me in
If you look around
You won't find
What you looked for

Don't Hesitate

I'm so in love with you
I know you can't deny
You really amaze me
What he wishes he could be
I know he'll miss you
Don't hesitate
You'll be in good hands
If you can't ignore the crowds
Do the things that she does
Just be happy when I'm not
Gonna be here all the time
I'm gonna be in love with you
Do it with me
You can do it with me
Don't delay
Don't hesitate
Don't hesitate
Do it with me
I used to be a common woman
I used to be normal
My reasons for wanting you
It's not the same as back in my young days
Remember how much I loved you
Now I bet this skin's changed my mind
Shed its love

Can't Believe It

And all we've got our fears and doubt
Just as long as the stars don't come out
And all we've got
Just wait and see
Until the wind is blowing
I won't be home no more
Can't believe it
You never did understand
Or wanted me
No other guy around
Or even Just stepped up in the ring
Don't know how I ever came into this
But I know that I've seen you now
I've seen you in my dreams
Now I'm here alone
So, you can make the day
I'll comfort you with a loving hand
Nothing to hide
And all we've got
Just wait and see
Until the wind is blowing
I won't be home no more
Can't believe it

Baby, Baby

That the way she smiles
But my heart will not forget you
And she'll hold you tight tonight
And I can't forget
No, I can't forget baby
Or you and me, oh girl, till the end
Baby, baby
Well, I need you and me
And I want the best
For you and me
For now
And I know
All I need's you and me
And then, once again
Baby, baby
I need you and me
Forgive me
If there's ever a moment
That makes you feel so right
In a kind of way
And then it's there
And I will never forget
Baby, baby
I need you and me
Let's get closer you baby

I Can't Live Without You

Gonna get in my way
I try, but the things I say can get really twisted
I'm gonna take my drugs
I'm gonna get in my time
I'm gonna do it I can't live without you
I'm gonna do it I can't live without you
I'm gonna do it I've got the blues right there, yeah
I'm gonna get in my way
I'm gonna be a better man
I'm gonna get in my way
Can't live without love
Like a pack of wolves in the breeze
I can't live without you
This pack will get you by, oh no
No more going to Hell
No more killing, I'm not gonna fight no more
I can't live without you
It can get me by me

Somebody Cries

It's not the story
No, it's not the song
It's not the way you have been
Oh, it's not the story
And it's not the song
It's not the way you have been
It's not the song
It's not the way you have been
Sometimes you're not for forever
Sometimes you're not right
I got no idea
If love is going to survive
And if happiness is going to survive
We'll keep the warmth inside,
Keep the storms dry
We'll keep the faith
We'll keep tomorrow
We'll keep tomorrow for real
Raindrops are fallin'
Somebody cries
I'm not cryin'
And baby I'm not yes, I care
If love is going to survive
And if happiness is going to survive

You Want to Be Kissed

If you want to get high
If you need to be kissed
If you're alone
Get drunk before you go
Think it over before you fall
Like there's no other way
You want some weight to lose
You want to be kissed
Get drunk before you fall
Think it over before you fall
Like there's no other way
You want some weight to lose
You want to be kissed
You want to be kissed
You want to be
You want some weight to lose
You want to be kissed
You want some weight to lose
Some weight to lose
We might be losing something in control
(What we're looking at today)

No Danger Baby

We'll all leave on our own free choice
It makes you come running home alone
Why don't you take little boy high up in your hand
It's not your fault he's so quiet
Why don't you take little boy high up in his hand
No danger baby
Ain't no need to talk
If you feel you're lonely
When you want to argue
Let the decision come to you
If you feel you're lonely
When you need to run away
Let the moment come when you need to run home
Why don't you take little boy high up in your hand
No danger baby
Ain't no need to walk
Don't wanna hear that little boy scream
Oh no no no
'Cause you make the call

To Love You Better

So why do I always look so evil?
I know I'll always look so bad if I think that you are my girl
I know I'll always look so bad
If I will believe
That I will need you always
It's not the way that you should be
I don't wanna pretend
That I am a fool anymore
Cause no matter how you try
I still can't escape it
No, I will never learn to erase
To love you better
I can't erase that I am a fool
I know I will never learn to erase
To love you better
I can't erase that I am a fool
Yeah, I will never learn to erase
To love you better
I can't erase that I am a fool
No, I will never learn to erase
To love you better

We've Got History

We are a house of cards, where two sides meet
For one hot night to rock every night way
The deck is stacked this way
We are a house of cards, where two sides meet
For one hot night to rock every night way
The deck is stacked this way
We are not just friends
We've got history
We have history on file
To trade and play
With death and the state
On the line it's like a vision that's romantic
A buddy with a friend in crime or a lifetime friend
A buddy with a friend in crime or a lifetime friend
That old lady on the corner
That old lady in the back
I know some a young cowboy like you
And I'm young as a man
Yeah, I lie awake at night

'Cause It Sounds Beautiful

I like you
I don't like you
Sometimes you're out in the rain
Just listen to the sound
Of your voice
Somewhere out in the night
You're caught inside of this machine
This is for women only
Do you need a man to lead you home
Do you really want to settle down
And settle down
And change the world now it's all for you
'Cause it sounds beautiful
And you feel the way we feel today
And it's up to you to show us how
Do you want to change the world
Do you really want to change it all for us
And do you want to change the world
Do you really want to change the world
Do you really want to change the world
'Cause it sounds beautiful

Promise It'll Last

To the other side of this mirror
We were the same
Blinded by the show
The only thing we knew
Was love had passed
And if I could hold on
It would allow for the rest
I'm not the one
Who's got the gravity
It's not that they wanna
Promise it'll last
But in this scene
We ain't got the gravity in the bank
Blinded by the show,
by the show
Some of us maybe not wanna
Promise it'll last
But in this scene
We ain't got the gravity in the bank
Blinded by the show,
by the show
Some of us maybe not wanna
Promise it'll last
But in this scene

Ismael S. Rodriguez Jr. is a writer, poet, artist, and origami artist. He is originally from Philadelphia, PA but currently lives in Oakland Park, FL. He is a U.S. Navy veteran who served during Desert Storm. He is dual diagnosed with schizophrenia and a substance abuse problem and has experienced periods of homelessness. He now has 15 years clean and sober and is mentally and emotionally stable and in treatment for his issues. He is an ordained reverend and a Grey Witch who is also interested in Discordianism and ceremonial magick. He has a website where he posts poems, short stories, origami, and other things. The website is at bulletproofpoet.com that link as well as other links can be found at https://linktr.ee/bulletproofpoet.